CATS ARE BETTER THAN MEN

Cats Are Better than Men

Beverly Guhl

Gramercy

New York

This 2002 edition is published by Gramercy Books™, an imprint of Random House Value Publishing, Inc., 280 Park Avenue, New York, NY 10017, by arrangement with The Doubleday Broadway Publishing Group, a division of Random House, Inc.

Gramercy Books™ and design are trademarks of Random House Value Publishing, Inc.

Printed in China.

Book design by Jennifer Ann Daddio

Random House
New York • Toronto • London • Sydney • Auckland
www.randomhouse.com

A catalog record for this title is available from the Library of Congress.

ISBN: 0-517-22094-6

9 8 7 6 5 4 3 2 1

To cats and men everywhere,
without whom this book could not have been written

CATS ARE BETTER THAN MEN

They never complain about your weight.

They never accuse you of being
too emotional.

They can show their emotions.

They take an interest in your work.

They never leave the seat up.

They don't care how much money you spend.

They don't use up all the hot water.

They don't need to see a shrink.

They always let you know when
they plan to go out.

They're eager to please you.

They never have other plans.

They heartily approve of your
taste in furnishings.

They don't complain about work
or their boss.

They don't talk about themselves.

They're Kissable, and there's
no beard burn.

They think you look just fine
without makeup.

They don't require closet space.

They don't cheat on you.

They listen to your problems.

They never try to make you
feel guilty.

They don't care what you wear to bed.

They don't eat up all the food
in the fridge.

They never say they'll call
then never call.

They LO_VE_ yard work.

They like to snuggle all night long.

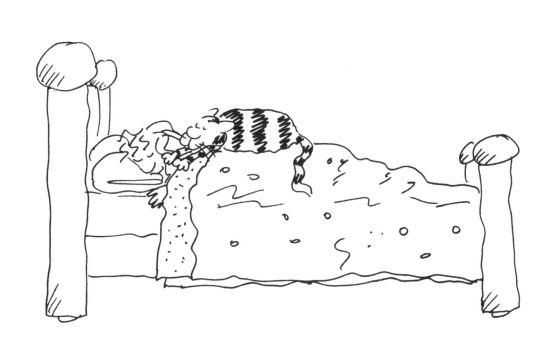

They never break dates at
the last minute.

They're never late for dinner.

Their grooming habits are
never in question.

They never complain about your cooking.

...or your friends...

...or your new hairdo.

They don't work weekends.

They never ask to borrow money.

They _LOVE_ leftovers.

They think you look wonderful
in the morning.

They can take care of themselves
when you go out.

They don't leave smelly socks
all over the house.

They never make you feel stupid.

They're always bringing you gifts.

They don't hide behind a newspaper.

They love your fuzzy terry
bathrobe as much as you do.

They don't care if you don't shave your legs for days or weeks.

They _LOVE_ your mother.

They have impeccable table manners.

They're never on the phone.

They like romance novels, too.

They never complain about your housekeeping.

They don't watch sports on TV.

They love dinner parties.

What a cute cat!
How affectionate!
Isn't this the sweetest kitty?!!
Is it OK to give the cat some salmon?

They don't hog the covers or snore.

Beverly Guhl has designed and marketed everything from greeting cards and stationary to decorative magnets, record albums, and mugs. She has also written and illustrated six other books: *Purrfect Parenting, Teenage Years—A Parent's Survival Guide, The Cat's Guide to Love, Cats are Better than Kids, Cats are Smarter than Men,* and *Cats are Smarter than Men, too!* The mother of two grown children and three cats—Brodie, Willis, and Travis—she lives in Austin, Texas.